1. Groot-Zundert, the Netherlands. Vincent van Gogh was born here in 1853. In the Dutch language, *groot* means "a large and spacious area." Today the town is usually just called Zundert. The Netherlands is a country that is sometimes called Holland.

2. London, England. As a young man, Vincent spent time here working at an art gallery.

3. The Borinage, Belgium. When Vincent was 25, he moved to this coal mining area to help poor families there.

4. Paris, France. Vincent decided to move to Paris, a major art center, to study art in 1886.

5. Arles, France. In 1888, Vincent left the busy city of Paris to paint in this sunny countryside village.

6. Saint-Rémy, France. Suffering from mental illness, Vincent entered a special hospital here, called an asylum, in 1889.

7. Auvers-sur-Oise, France. Vincent van Gogh traveled to Auvers in 1890. He would spend the last few weeks of his life there. In French, *Auvers-sur-Oise* means "Auvers on the Oise River."

TIMELINE OF VINCENT VAN GOGH'S LIFE

 1853 Vincent van Gogh is born in Groot-Zundert.

 1868 At age 15, Vincent abruptly leaves school. The next year, his uncle gets him a job as a sales clerk at Groupils art gallery.

1873 Vincent is transferred to the London branch of Groupils. He loves the art he sees there, and begins writing letters to his family. He draws pictures to show his family what London looks like.

 1876 Vincent leaves his gallery job and tries teaching.

 1877 A restless Vincent van Gogh leaves his teaching job. He tries working in a bookstore, and then decides to become a clergyman, or minister, like his father.

 1878 Vincent travels to the Borinage, Belgium. He wants to help the poor miners and their families. He draws and sketches the people he meets there.

THIS WAY

1880 Drawing becomes more and more important to Vincent. Finally, at age 27, he decides to become an artist!

 1886 Vincent moves to Paris. He meets the Impressionist artists and loves their work. He starts painting his first self-portraits.

 **1888** Vincent leaves Paris and travels to Arles. A few months later, his friend Paul Gauguin joins him. Vincent begins his famous sunflower paintings.

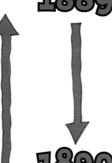 **1889** After a terrible argument with Gauguin, Vincent becomes so depressed he enters an asylum. While being treated there, he creates some of his finest paintings, including *The Starry Night*.

 1890 Vincent moves to Auvers-sur-Oise, just north of Paris, where is he cared for by his friend, Dr. Gachet. Vincent continues painting right up to the end of his life. He dies in Auvers on July 29, at the age of 37.

  UP HERE

GETTING TO KNOW THE WORLD'S GREATEST ARTISTS

VINCENT
VAN GOGH

WRITTEN AND ILLUSTRATED BY MIKE VENEZIA

CHILDREN'S PRESS®

An Imprint of Scholastic Inc.

New York Toronto London Auckland Sydney
Mexico City New Delhi Hong Kong
Danbury, Connecticut

Dedicated to George and Anne
A special thanks to Sarah Mollman

Cover: *Sunflowers* (1888 or 1889), Oil on Canvas.
© The Philadelphia Museum of Art, The Mr. and Mrs. Carroll S. Tyson, Jr.,
Collection/Art Resource, NY

Library of Congress Cataloging-in-Publication Data

Venezia, Mike, author, illustrator.
[Van Gogh]
 Vincent van Gogh / by Mike Venezia.—Revised Edition.
    pages cm.—(Getting to know the world's greatest artists)
 Includes index.
 ISBN 978-0-531-21978-2 (library binding)—
 ISBN 978-0-531-22539-4 (pbk.)
 1. Gogh, Vincent van, 1853-1890—Juvenile literature. I. Title.

ND653.G7V46 2014
759.9492—dc23
[B]   2014014732

1 2 3 4 5 6 7 8 9 10 R 24 23 22 21 20 19 18 17 16 15

Self Portrait. 1886-1887. Panel, 41.0 x 32.5 cm. © 1988 The Art Institute of Chicago

Vincent van Gogh was one of the most tragic artists who ever lived. Nothing ever seemed to go right for him and he wasn't very happy. He never even smiled in his self-portraits.

Van Gogh was born in Holland in 1853 and died in France in 1890. Unlike most artists, van Gogh didn't decide to become a painter until he was grown up.

He tried a lot of other things first.

He worked in an art gallery selling
paintings. He tried teaching. He
worked in a bookstore and he was a
preacher like his dad.

None of these things made him
very happy. Then one day he decided
to be an artist.

(top left) *Miners.* 1880. Pencil, 17½ x 22 cm. State Museum Kröller-Müller, Otterlo, the Netherlands

(top right) *Peasant Walking with Stick.* 1885. Black chalk, 13½ x 7½ cm. State Museum Kröller-Müller, Otterlo, the Netherlands

(bottom) *Sand Pit with Men at Work.* 1883. Pencil. Vincent Van Gogh Foundation/ National Museum Vincent Van Gogh, Amsterdam

Van Gogh always tried his best at whatever he did, so he went to different art schools to learn everything he could about drawing and painting. His early drawings were of the poor people he used to help when he was a preacher.

Sien with Child on Lap. 1883. Black chalk, 16¼ x 17¼ cm.
State Museum Kröller-Müller, Otterlo, the Netherlands

On the Road. 1881. Black chalk. Vincent Van Gogh Foundation/
National Museum Vincent Van Gogh, Amsterdam

There are certain things you can
see in these drawings that show up
later in his famous paintings, such as
the strong lines and shapes. You can
see the feelings he had for everyday
people.

Potato Eaters, Nuenun. 1885. Oil on canvas.
Vincent Van Gogh, Foundation/National Museum Vincent Van Gogh, Amsterdam

Van Gogh's first paintings were also of the poor people he had been helping. In this painting, the family was so poor they had only a few potatoes to eat for dinner. They look tired and not very happy.

Two Women in the Peat. 1883. Oil on canvas.
Vincent Van Gogh Foundation/National Museum Vincent Van Gogh, Amsterdam

The colors in van Gogh's early paintings are dark and sad.

He wanted everyone to know how hard the lives of the poor people were.

Van Gogh kept using dark colors until he discovered some very colorful Japanese artwork. He loved the bright colors and strong lines and shapes that he saw.

Farmhouse in Provence, Arles. 1888. Oil on canvas. National Gallery of Art, Washington, D.C.

Soon van Gogh's paintings started to look much more colorful.

Look at the difference between the gloomy *Potato Eaters* and the painting above, which was done only a few years later.

We know a lot about how van Gogh felt, and why he did certain things, because he was always writing letters to his younger brother, Theo.

Theo always helped his brother. He encouraged him to paint and sent him money when he could.

The Postman Roulin, Arles. 1889. Oil on canvas.
State Museum Kröller-Müller, Otterlo, the Netherlands

Because van Gogh was always
sending and receiving letters, he got
to know his postman pretty well. He
painted pictures of him and used the
postman's wife as a model in many of
his paintings as well.

In 1886 Vincent moved to Paris, France, to join Theo.

Paris was the center of the art world then. Since Theo was in the business of buying and selling paintings, and Vincent wanted to be an artist, it seemed like a pretty good place to be.

Theo introduced Vincent to a lot of painters while they lived in Paris.

Hardly anyone knew it then, but
many of those painters would
become world-famous artists
someday.

A couple of years later, Vincent van Gogh decided to leave Paris and move to a small country town called Arles.

Van Gogh thought Arles would be a great place for artists to get together to paint and talk about their different ideas. He tried very hard to get as many artists as he could to join him. The only one to try it out was Paul Gauguin, although he wasn't really crazy about the idea.

It turned out to be a big mistake.

Gauguin didn't seem to like
anything van Gogh did in Arles.
They argued a lot.

Van Gogh probably decided to listen to Gauguin about cleaning the place up, because his bedroom looks pretty neat in this painting.

Bedroom at Arles. 1888. Oil on canvas, 73.6 x 92.3 cm. © 1988 The Art Institute of Chicago

Finally, after a very bad argument, Gauguin decided to leave van Gogh and return to Paris.

Van Gogh didn't know what to do. He really wanted things to work out well with Gauguin.

Van Gogh had always had problems during his life with the way he felt. Sometimes he would get so angry and upset that no one could make him feel better. This time he became so angry and upset he cut off part of his ear!

Self-Portrait with Bandaged Ear. 1889. Oil on canvas. Courtauld Institute Galleries, London

Van Gogh painted pictures of himself after this happened.

It looks like he wished he hadn't done it.

Vincent van Gogh never really got better after Gauguin left him.

The Starry Night. 1889. Oil on Canvas, 73.7 x 92.1 cm. The Museum of Modern Art, New York

Sometimes he was too angry to paint, and sometimes he was too sad to paint. When he felt good, he painted better than ever.

He made the stars in *The Starry Night* seem like they're really shining.

Cypresses. 1889. Oil on canvas, 93.3 x 74 cm. The Metropolitan Museum of Art, New York

The trees in this painting look like flames, and it feels like the whole picture is moving.

In this painting van Gogh made the sun look really hot. You almost feel like you should put sunglasses on to look at it.

Olive Trees. 1889. Oil on canvas. The Minneapolis Institute of Arts

Detail, *Sunflowers*. 1888. Oil on canvas. Scala/ Art Resource

Van Gogh usually put his paint on very thick. Sometimes he painted so fast he didn't even mix his colors. He used paint right out of the tube.

Van Gogh used so much paint he was always running out. Sometimes he stopped buying food in order to buy more paint, so he was hungry a lot of the time, and he wasn't healthy.

Hardly anyone was interested in van Gogh's work while he was alive. He sold only a few drawings and maybe one or two paintings. People in the 1880s and 1890s just weren't used to the bright "moving" pictures that van Gogh made.

Today things are different. People have learned how beautiful Vincent van Gogh's art is.

Now his paintings are some of the most popular in the world.

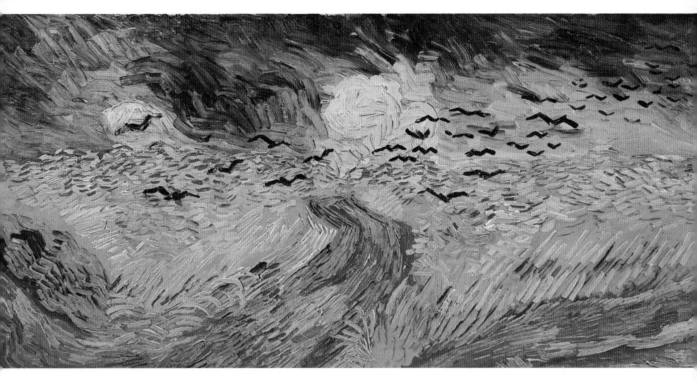

Wheatfield with Crows. 1890. Oil on canvas.
Vincent Van Gogh Foundation/National Museum Vincent Van Gogh, Amsterdam

This may have been van Gogh's last painting. Some people think it shows how angry and upset he must have been feeling because he painted a scary sky, roads that led to a dark background, and crows that look like bats.

Soon after this painting was finished, van Gogh shot himself. He died two days later.

Van Gogh made
his paintings seem
alive with color.
His colors are
so bright and
beautiful you can
almost smell
the flowers he
painted, or feel
the bright sun.

Sunflowers. 1888. Oil on canvas. Scala/Art Resource

*Garden of
the Poets.
1888.
Oil on canvas,
73 x 92.1 cm.
© 1988, The Art
Institute
of Chicago*

His brush strokes
give everything a
feeling of movement.
Trees, stars, and
people feel alive.

L'Arlesienne. 1888. Oil on canvas. 91.4 x 73.7 cm.
The Metropolitan Museum of Art, New York

ive Grove. 1889. Oil on canvas.
te Museum Kröller-Müller, Otterlo, the Netherlands

Maybe more than
any other artist,
van Gogh's feelings
came out in his
paintings. That's why
Vincent van Gogh
is one of the world's
greatest artists.

It's much better to see a real Vincent van Gogh painting than a picture of one. It's fun to see how thick he put his paint on, his brush strokes, and how bright his colors are.

The pictures in this book came from the museums listed below. If none of them is close to you, maybe you can visit one when you are on vacation.

The Art Institute of Chicago
Courtauld Institute Galleries, London
The Metropolitan Museum of Art, New York
The Minneapolis Institute of Arts
The Museum of Modern Art, New York
National Gallery of Art, Washington, D.C.
State Museum Kröller-Müller, Otterlo, the Netherlands
Vincent Van Gogh Foundation / National Museum Vincent Van Gogh, Amsterdam
Yale University Art Gallery, New Haven, Connecticut

LEARN MORE BY TAKING THE VAN GOGH QUIZ!

(ANSWERS ON THE NEXT PAGE.)

1. Why did some bright yellows and reds in Vincent van Gogh's paintings darken or fade a few years after he finished the paintings?

a Because Vincent added mustard and strawberry syrup to his yellow and red paints to make them go farther.

b Because Vincent could afford only cheap, low-quality paint that faded and changed over time.

c Art gallery owners thought van Gogh's colors were too bright for their customers to enjoy, so they covered certain areas of his paintings with dull, boring colors.

2. During his life, Vincent sold one painting, *Red Vineyard at Arles*, for about $80. Today his paintings sell for:

a $85 each

b A million dollars each

c Millions and millions and millions of dollars each

3. Besides Dutch, what languages did Vincent speak?

a German

b Klingon

c English

d French

4. Vincent van Gogh signed only a few of his paintings because:

a He often forgot how to spell his name.

b He only signed the paintings he thought were his very best.

c The president of France didn't like Vincent's name.

5. Vincent often had only one meal a day. What did he usually eat?

a Dry bread and coffee

b Dry bread and a small bowl of oatmeal

c Just dry bread

d A yogurt smoothie

6. How many letters did Vincent write to his brother, Theo?

a 16

b Around 800

c 24,000

ANSWERS

1. **b** Vincent used inexpensive paint, so chemical reactions from heat, paint additives, and varnish coatings caused some colors in his paintings to fade. But don't worry. Today art restorers have been able to bring many of Vincent's favorite colors back to their original brightness!

2. **c** Over the last few years, a number of Vincent's paintings have sold for a total of over 700 million dollars!

3. **a, c, and d** Vincent was very good at learning languages. Besides Dutch, Vincent spoke German, English and French.

4. **b** Vincent van Gogh only signed paintings that really satisfied him. He signed just 130 paintings out of about 900.

Also, he signed his paintings "Vincent," not "Vincent van Gogh," because he said that most people in France couldn't pronounce "van Gogh" correctly.

5. **a, b, or c** Vincent ate skimpy meals for a couple of reasons. One was that he wanted to live exactly like the poor coal miners he was helping. Later in his life, he just couldn't afford a good meal. Vincent spent what little money he had on paint and on paying models to sit for his paintings.

6. **b** Vincent van Gogh wrote more than 800 letters to his friends and family. Most of them were to Theo. Because of these letters, people know a lot of information about Vincent van Gogh.

HEY, WHAT DOES THAT WORD MEAN?

art gallery (ART GAL-uh-ree) A place where artwork is displayed and sometimes sold

background (BAK-ground) The part of a picture that is behind the main subject

brush strokes (BRUHSH STROHKS) The mark that an artist makes on a painting with a paintbrush

encourage (en-KUR-ij) To give someone confidence by praising or supporting the person

preacher (PREECH-uhr) A minister of religion

self-portrait (SELF POR-trit) A drawing, painting, or photograph of oneself

tragic (TRAJ-ik) Extremely unfortunate, sad, or disastrous

Visit this Scholastic Web site for more information on Vincent van Gogh: www.factsfornow.scholastic.com
Enter the keywords Vincent van Gogh

INDEX